Darrin Gee, Spirit of Golf Academy

"The Spirit of Golf is essential to the game of the seasoned
professional as well as the beginning golfer."
PGA Tour Champion Jerry Kelly

Ranked among the top golf schools in America
by GOLF Magazine

Recommended by Frommer's Travel Guides

PRAISE FOR
*The Seven Principles of Golf: Mastering the Mental Game
On and Off the Golf Course*

"This book belongs on your golf bookshelf next to Harvey
Penick's *Little Red Book* and Ben Hogan's *Five Lessons.*"
Barnes & Noble Editors

"A poignant, common-sense approach to golf that can point
the way to a better game and a better life."
Brian McCallen, *Golf's Best New Destinations* and
Golf Magazine's Top 100 Courses You Can Play

A Top Five Golf Book in New England by *The Boston Globe*

PRAISE FOR
*The Seven Personalities of Golf: Discover Your Inner
Golfer to Play Your Best Game*

Excerpt featured in the July 2009 issue of GOLF Magazine,
"The New Way to Manage Your Game"

Library of Congress Cataloging-in-Publication Data
Gee, Darrin
The frustrated golfer's handbook : 50 mental golf tricks to get you back on
course...fast / Darrin Gee.
p. cm.
1. Golf. 2. Golf—Psychological aspects. I. Title.
2014904196

ISBN 978-0975431696
eBook ISBN 978-0975431627

Published in the United States of America

Book design by Matthew Pearce

ALSO BY DARRIN GEE

THE FRUSTRATED GOLFER'S HANDBOOK

50 Mental Golf Tricks to Get You Back on Course...Fast

DARRIN GEE

CONTENTS

PART II: ON THE DRIVING RANGE & PUTTING GREEN

HOW TO PERFECT YOUR GRIP

HOW TO PERFECT YOUR BALANCE

Introduction

There is nothing more frustrating than hitting a perfect drive down the middle of the fairway and flubbing your next shot into the trees or a sand trap. Or what about getting a birdie on the toughest hole on the course and following it on the next hole with a double bogey? Even more frustrating is this: playing the best round of your life one day and then shooting twenty strokes higher the next time you're out.

Frustrated golfers know they're capable of hitting good shots—that's what makes it all so frustrating. You know you are capable of playing brilliantly for a hole or two. You know you are capable of putting it all together for a perfect round. However, you aren't able to do it consistently...until now.

There's one simple thing keeping you from playing your best golf. It's not your swing or the equipment or your fitness or your experience level. It's your MIND. Golf is 90% mental. That means that most of your mis-hits, penalties and high scores are caused by mental errors.

Many golfers say to themselves, "Don't hit it in the water, don't hit it in the water, please don't hit it in the water!" Guess where the ball usually ends up? In the water! Some people are so flustered by a group waiting behind them that they can't seem to pause for a couple seconds to make a solid swing. Others get so nervous on the first tee that they're as stiff as a corpse.

Or maybe you play great golf on the driving range, but can't seem to replicate it on the golf course. It's no problem playing by yourself, but your game falters or falls apart when you play with strangers. But technically nothing has changed in these scenarios. Same golf course, same conditions, same clubs, same ball. The only thing that has changed is your frame of mind.

How to Use This Book

What sets top performers apart from everyone else is that they commit to developing their mental game—they learn how to get out of their own way.

The mental golf tricks in this book will help you do what you are already capable of doing—hitting great shots on a consistent basis. This book provides simple tips and practical advice to help you eliminate distractions and reduce anxiety while increasing your focus, concentration and relaxation. I know these tricks work because each one has been tested and proven at my top-rated Spirit of Golf Academy on the Island of Hawaii by golfers just like you.

The exercises are designed to address different situations you may face before, during or after a round of golf. Golf is a game of ebb and flow, so understanding the tools at your disposal will ensure that they're available to you whenever—and wherever—you need them.

Get ready, because these mental golf tricks will take your game to the next level. You'll overcome your frustrations, enjoy your time on the course, and feel confident that you're playing your very best. They'll help you regardless of your ability or experience—I've seen beginning and professional golfers benefit from these tricks. Using *even one* of these mental golf tricks will result in improvement in your game.

Let's get started!

PART I

ON THE GOLF COURSE

1

How to Overcome First Tee Jitters: Go Sloooooow

First tee jitters. Just the thought of the first tee can cause tension and stress in a golfer. This unfortunately translates into tightness in your swing.

A great trick to start your round off on the right note is to *go slow.* Slow down everything. Walk slower, talk slower, breath slower, move slower, think slower. Though it may seem as if you are moving at a snail's pace, in reality you will most likely be moving at a normal, regular speed.

By consciously slowing down your actions and thoughts, you will be able to manage your heart rate, blood pressure, adrenaline level, and breathing. Your body will be better equipped to handle the pressure and your swing will be more relaxed.

I was the special guest at a large charity golf tournament fundraiser. From the moment I arrived, I was on the go—taking pictures with participants and celebrities, conducting a mini-clinic, coaching golfers individually and preparing for the awards banquet in which I would be the keynote speaker. On top of all this,

I was playing in the golf tournament.

Even though I wasn't able to follow my regular pre-round ritual, I utilized the *go slow* trick not only on the first tee but also throughout the entire day. As a result, I was able to move at my normal, regular pace. With so many different responsibilities, you would think the last thing I could do is play decent golf. As it turned out, I played one of my best rounds of the year.

The next time you feel nervous or stressed on the first tee or when the pressure is on, remember to go slow to relax and play great golf.

2

How to Tee Off in Front of a Crowd: Single-Pointed Focus

For the average golfer, teeing off in front of a crowd can be one of the most intimidating encounters on the golf course. Even if it's only one stranger who's watching, the most gifted of golfers can tighten up.

To overcome this type of distraction, consciously shift your focus. Single-pointed focus is dedicating all of your attention towards one thing. I focus on my abdomen, in particular to a spot two inches below my belly button where my belt buckle is located.

In martial arts, this area of the body is called the *hara* or lower *dantian*. Many believe this is the center of your body where your energy and power emanates. Shift your attention to this area of your body to eliminate mental distractions such as strangers watching, hazards and extraneous thoughts off the golf course.

Give this a try on the driving range. Hit ten shots your usual way. Then, on the next ten, focus only on the spot two inches below your belly button. Notice if this centering or single-pointed focus helps you hit higher quality shots. You may notice that you are able to hit the sweet spot more consistently, resulting in more solid shots that go where you want them to go.

Next try it on the golf course, especially when people are watching. Focus on a single-point until the distractions begin to dissipate and blur away. Then in your mind, it becomes just you, the ball and your target. Swing away.

If you find your attention wandering during a round of golf such as thinking about something at work or home or being distracted by the beauty of the surroundings or thinking too much about performance and swing mechanics, utilize this single-pointed focus to eliminate these and other distractions.

3

How to Hit Over Water: 911 Emergency

When a person is engaged in a 911 emergency situation, he or she focuses on the emergency with full attention. If a family member has a heart attack or is choking, you would respond instantaneously. You don't think about it; you act immediately. You don't take the time to turn off the TV or put away your meal in the refrigerator or finish the chore you were doing. You stop and focus. In fact, you focus ALL of your attention.

When hitting a critical shot, treat the event like a 911 situation. Some may consider this extreme. It is perhaps, however, I believe that the majority of the world's top golfers are able to employ this level of focus and concentration when it counts.

You don't have to do this for every shot. Most of us would not be able to do that. However, it is a great tool to have in your arsenal when you need it, such as hitting a tee shot over water to a green. You can turn on the 911 signal to close out a match. If you need to hit a great shot to win a tournament, this trick can be powerful. Focus on the shot with your full attention. Don't allow distractions to pull your energy away from the moment.

If you find yourself hitting shot after shot on the driving range without purpose, stop and treat the next one as if your life depended on it. Train yourself to use this trick on the golf course under the most challenging of situations.

As you learn this trick, apply it periodically. Then see if you can do it more and more in each successive round. Soon, you will be able to use it on command when it counts.

4

How to Not Choke: Breathe

I often tell my students to imagine playing a round of golf with Tiger Woods in front of thousands of people with cameras broadcasting your every move to millions of viewers around the world. With the simple thought of being in such a situation, a golfer's mind and body reacts. Tension and stress build. Thoughts of possible embarrassment, nervousness and fright cause the golfer's body to tighten up.

How can you overcome something like this?

Breathe.

A no-brainer, right? Wrong. The human body has a built-in self-preservation mechanism that responds to environmental changes. For example, if you sense danger, your heart rate, adrenaline and blood pressure increase automatically so that your body can react and respond.

This may be useful in a fight-or-flight situation, however in the game of golf, it can be detrimental. On the golf course, feelings of fear, discomfort, apprehension, nervousness or insecurity can lead to negative physical affects including shortness of breath. This sets off a chain reaction. Shortness of breath leads to oxygen deprivation, which then causes tension and tightness in your muscles. When muscles tense up, they do not perform optimally.

In competitive sports, you often hear the word "choke" used to describe an athlete who self-destructs under duress or at critical moments of a competition. I believe that "choking" is perhaps a literal description of what happens. If an athlete becomes distracted by extraneous thoughts, he or she loses the ability to play freely. Perhaps he or she begins to think about collecting the championship trophy or how he or she better not blow a lead. The athlete becomes self-conscious and begins to analyze and observe his or her own actions, which often leads to poor performance.

Once this happens, the body's self-preservation or fight-or-flight mechanism kicks in. Heart rate increases, blood pressure increases and adrenaline increases. Along with this comes shortness of breath. In other words, the athlete literally chokes him or herself.

What happens next is perplexing to most athletes. They feel as if they are going through their usual motions and movements, however their bodies are unable to respond accordingly. The perceived same swing results in off-center hits. The perceived same jump shot in basketball clanks off the backboard or is an air ball.

If this happens to you, simply breathe to maintain or return to a higher level of performance. Not all breaths are created equal. Because your adrenaline level and heart rate have increased, you need a breathing technique that will slow you down and return you to an optimal state of performance. A deep, cleansing breath is needed.

Breathe deep into your abdomen. This is often called a diaphragmatic, belly or yogic breath. When you inhale, the lungs will fill with air, forcing your diaphragm downwards which makes your belly protrude outward. When you maximize your lung capacity, it will feel as if your belly is fully expanded.

While it is important to inhale fully, the pacing of your breathing is just as important. Break down a breath into four parts: 1) inhale into your abdomen slowly for a count of four seconds, 2) transition or rest for four seconds, 3) exhale slowly for four seconds, and 4) transition or rest for four seconds. The number of seconds is arbitrary. For some it will be more and others less. You will begin to increase your oxygen levels leading to a higher level of energy and focus allowing you to perform at your best, even while playing with Tiger Woods in front of thousands of viewers.

5

How to Shoot a Hole-in-One: Shrink the Green

If you have the desire to shoot a hole-in-one, you must focus on one thing and only one thing while standing on the tee—the hole. Eliminate all distractions—sand traps, water, trees, wind, scenery, wildlife—and focus on the true target.

I took a seasoned player out on the golf course for a nine-hole playing lesson. He was a single digit handicapper who had the potential to play professionally. He could work the ball on command and had the ability to hit just about every shot possible. However, every now and then, he went astray. He lost focus. He would step up to the ball and just swing, without a true intention or goal. I told him that if he desired to play to his true potential, he would need to up-level his focus.

This mental golf trick is most applicable to approaching greens, in particular on par-3's. When looking at the green, divide it into quadrants. Observe which quadrant the flag is located. In your mind, shrink the green and direct your focus to the quadrant with the flag. As you practice this trick, you can shrink the quadrant to smaller areas—ideally to the size of the hole. Direct all your focus towards that specific target to increase your chance of shooting a hole-in-one.

6

How to Hit More Greens:
Take One More Club

I enjoy observing how golfers operate on the golf course. You can learn a lot about a person. One of the most interesting processes I enjoy watching is how each individual golfer determines what club to hit.

Some march out their distances by counting each and every step. Others use range view finders. Some look for the 150-yard marker and gauge their distance accordingly. Some just go with instinct. Into the calculation goes wind speed and direction, elevation change, pin placement and for some the sun and the moon. All kidding aside, a golfer ultimately determines the distance from the ball to the target and then selects the club that he or she believes will hit the ball that distance.

However, the majority of golfers pick a club that they have to hit perfectly to go the specific distance. In other words, if they don't hit it just right, the ball more than likely falls short. In fact, for the majority of amateurs, when they miss their target they miss it short. It's because of a slight miscalculation.

Alternatively, determine the club that you want to hit as usual, and then add one extra. For example, if you select an 8-iron for a shot, add one more club and hit a 7-iron instead. Then proceed with the same pre-shot ritual or routine as usual.

If you hit it less than perfect, the ball will still go far enough to the chosen target. If you hit it poorly, the ball could still be on the green but a little short. If you hit it perfectly, the ball may end up a little long but it will most likely be on or around the green. In most cases, you will most likely be on or around the green. Try this little trick to hit more greens and ultimately shoot more birdies and pars.

7

How to Make Every Putt:
Pick the Blade of Grass

On the putting green, I commonly ask my students, "What do you want?" The answers I hear often are "I want to get it close" or "I don't want to three-putt" or "I just want to get within three feet." It is interesting how few actually say, "I want the ball in the hole." Many people miss this seemingly simple part of the game. Golfers become so focused on peripheral issues, such as making a perfect stroke or not slowing down play or avoiding a three-putt, that they lose sight of the true goal—getting the ball in the hole.

Putt with the intention of making it. Visualize the ball rolling over a *specific blade* of grass at the cup and into the hole. The ball could technically go in anywhere around the hole—all 360 degrees of the hole. It could go in the front, side or even roll past the hole and back toward you, going into the *back* of the hole.

In *The Seven Principles of Golf,* the third principle "Visualize the Shot" discusses the three steps to successful visualization:

1. knowing what you want,

2. seeing it in your mind's eye, and
3. trusting and committing 100%.

After determining what you want (getting the ball in the hole), visualize the line (or path of the ball from start to finish, including the blade of grass at the hole). The more detail you include, the higher chance of making the putt. This will increase your confidence and you will learn how to trust and commit to your line 100%. This in turn will increase your chance of creating the putt that you want, over the blade of grass and into the hole.

8

How to Handle Pressure: Break it Up

You will most likely feel pressure on the golf course at some point in your golfing life. It may be on the first tee or hitting a shot in front of a small crowd or playing to an island green or standing over a 15-foot putt to win the Masters. No matter your level of play, from pure beginners to the greatest players of all time, golfers will feel some pressure on the golf course—that's a given. How you deal with and handle the pressure is what determines your true character.

Everyone is different. Each individual has a unique personality, style and demeanor both on and off the golf course. In *The Seven Personalities of Golf*, I discuss how each person can identify his or her dominant personality or style on the golf course and more importantly, learn how to maximize natural tendencies for a higher level of performance. This can also include toning it down at certain times to perform at your best.

For example, the Swashbuckler personality describes golfers who usually attack pins and take on high-risk strategies even when they might not need to do so (i.e., standing on the last tee of a major championship with a two-stroke lead). In a situation such as this, a golfer with the Swashbuckler personality can play conservatively, even settling for a par or bogey in a worst-case scenario, rather than going for an unnecessary birdie that brings in the risk of a potentially disastrous outcome.

Each of us handles pressure uniquely. Some people perform better when no one is around. Some are the exact opposite and need the presence of playing partners in a competitive environment in order to thrive. Ideal situations, whatever they may be, are not always possible.

When you are feeling pressure on the golf course, think of something that makes you perform at your best. For the majority of golfers, being relaxed and calm leads to their best performances. In these cases, taking a deep, deep breath into the abdomen and then exhaling slowly will have a calming effect (Mental Golf Trick #4). Others might sing or hum a tune. One of my clients used a mantra, repeating the words, "Easy does it." It helped him do exactly that. Some have told me that they use prayer to stay calm.

Another way to break up the pressure is to smile and laugh every now and then. Think of something funny to break up the intensity. You can also do something physical such as shaking your arms and legs loose or doing a stretch. Many yoga and tai chi movements and stances are designed to release tension and balance out your internal energy. I don't expect you to get on the ground or strike a pose that feels awkward or out of place, but perhaps you can do something that is more subtle and unnoticeable to everyone else, yet allows you to relax and handle the pressure.

As mentioned above, for some golfers and their personalities, they may need to increase the pressure by doing the opposite, such as pressing or doubling a bet when they're about to lose. This may get them more motivated in a pressure situation leading to a higher level of performance.

No matter which situation describes you, the key is to break up the pressure and turn it into a positive outcome. Determine what works best for you and use it on the golf course to see how you can perform well under all conditions.

9

How to Relax When Being Rushed: Be Ready and Then Slow Down

Let's face it—golfers can be jerks. Have you ever been enjoying a nice leisurely round and up from behind charges a group that's on pace for a sub-three hour round? It's as if they're sprinting up and down the fairways. Some stand on the fairway behind you with their hands on their hips, while others wave their clubs as if they are flagging down a rescue plane.

When feeling rushed, many people begin to panic. They get jittery and begin to rubberneck. They look back at the group behind them over and over again. When they finally get to their ball, they are so distracted by the group behind, that they barely pause before swinging which results in poor shots and lower performance.

There's a simple way to combat those sprinters behind you. If you do feel like you are playing slowly, pick up the pace. In fact, if you'd like, go ahead and rush or even run. However, only do this *between* your shots. When it's your turn to hit, stop, slow down and play at your optimum pace.

The thing that slows down the game of golf is not the two seconds during a golf swing or even the set-up and pre-shot ritual. Those take time, but what actually slows the game down is not being ready to hit when it's your turn.

"Oh, is it my shot? Sorry, let me get a club. Hmmm, what should I hit here? I think I need to march off the distance. Wait, it's windy, I need to change clubs." Does this sound familiar? This is what slows the game down. Be ready to hit your shot when it's your turn and then you can start your pre-shot ritual at your own pace and rhythm. You'll make a better shot and save time in the long run.

10

How to Play with Strangers: Block Them Out

"I hate playing with strangers!"

I hear this all the time from my clients. I always ask them, "Why?" and the usual answers I get are:

"I don't want to embarrass myself."

"I don't want to slow them down."

"I can't relax."

"Golf is nerve wracking enough as it is, I don't need someone I don't know to add to the pressure."

"I don't want people to see how poorly I play."

"I want to play fast and others are going to slow me down."

"I don't want any distractions."

The interesting thing about golf is that if it's not a stranger that's distracting you, it's going to be something else. Rarely are you completely alone, without distractions on the golf course. For those who are nervous about playing with strangers, business associates, bosses, or any person that makes you feel uncomfortable, use this mental golf trick to overcome your nerves: block them out.

Imagine yourself inside a bubble or cocoon when it's time to hit your shot. This trick will allow you to focus solely on the shot at hand and eliminate extraneous information and distractions. This is a great tool for reducing the stress you might feel when you are distracted by the thought of playing golf with strangers. Once you hit your shot, in your mind allow the bubble to dissipate.

Try this out one shot at a time and after a few holes, you will feel much more relaxed and quite possibly begin enjoying the company of your playing partners.

11

How to Play Under the Weather:
Play the Cards You are Dealt

Every day is not created equal. Some days are sunny, some are cloudy. Some days are windy and others dead calm. The weather and course conditions are out of your control and constantly changing.

Likewise, you don't feel the same everyday. One day, you may feel strong and agile, the next day tired and lethargic. Another time, you are excited and enthusiastic, the next time bored and uninterested.

However, no matter the weather, course conditions or your demeanor, you still seem to end up on the first tee. The key to playing your best under all circumstances is to accept the situation at hand and adapt.

One of the best mental golf tricks to use when you face less-than-ideal conditions is to grip down on the club and swing easy. Even if you're not at 100% physically, you can still be at 100% mentally. Be smart. Play strategically. You can still strike the ball solidly and play great golf.

Many people tell me how they have played rounds of golf when they were sick or had recently strained a muscle. Because of their ailment, they were forced to physically tone down their efforts. Contrary to logic, less effort led to playing their best rounds ever.

The same applies to adverse conditions. I love playing in poor weather, because I immediately change my game plan and philosophy. I become the ultimate tactician, planning my way about the course. I take score out of the equation and focus on hitting quality shots one at a time. If the wind is gusting at 35 miles per hour, I change my game plan. I hit a lot of knockdown shots and bump-and-runs. Adapt to conditions, play the hand you're dealt and enjoy the game.

- HOW TO READ GREENS -

12

How to See the Break: Go with the Flow

Many golfers tell me they can't read greens and that it is very difficult for them to tell which direction the ball will curve when they're putting.

One mental golf trick that I recommend is to imagine that the green is made of cement. If you poured a bucket of water on it, imagine which direction the water would flow. If the water sits still, then the green is perfectly flat. If it flows in a certain direction, then the green is sloped accordingly.

When you hit the ball, it will roll with the flow of the water. This translates into the ball "breaking" on the green. Another way to look at this is to imagine standing on a riverbank with the water flowing from your left to the right. If you were to throw a leaf into the river, which direction would the leaf go? It would flow to the right.

So, if you imagine water flowing left to right on a putting green, that means the ball will flow (or curve) in that direction. Thus, when you visualize your putt, see the ball starting to the left of the hole so that it eventually rolls to the right and into the cup.

- HOW TO READ GREENS -

13

How to See the Path:
Red Light, Green Light

Simple is best, a philosophy that I believe strongly applies to golf. The key to reading greens is visualizing the ball going into the hole.

When I visualize, I see a fuzzy white line about the width of the ball that starts from the ball's resting position and goes along the ground on the path that I believe the ball will follow all the way into the cup. It looks like the lines that a TV sports commentator might draw on the screen. The Golf Channel and other networks often show the path of the ball with the same fuzzy line that I've been imagining for years.

Here are some of my favorite visualizations that my students have shared with me over the years:

- **Red light, green light**: a 6-year-old girl took our golf clinic and told me that she visualized in colors. If the line she saw was red, that meant, "Stop, don't hit the ball." Then she said she would wait for the line to turn green which meant, "Go" and she would hit the ball into the hole. She made 19 out of 20 putts from various distances using this technique.

- **Fishing line:** an avid fly fisherman visualized fishing line along the ground, which was the path of the ball into the hole.

- **Stitch line:** a quilter took our clinic and said that she imagined a stitch line sewn into the ground all the way into the hole.

- **Trough:** one golfer visualized the blades of grass parting and creating a trough that led to the hole. All she had to do was hit the ball and it would follow the trough to the bottom of the cup.

- **Railroad tracks:** some golfers have visualized the ball rolling on toy railroad tracks all the way into the hole. In the 1986 US Open at Shinnecock Hills in New York, Raymond Floyd said that he not only saw the tracks, but the train on the tracks shooting up puffs of smoke. Some of his visualizations were so vivid that they ironically became a distraction that caused him to step back from a few putts and start the pre-shot process again. His ability to see the path of the ball so vividly helped him win the championship.

- **Computer golf:** for those who have played golf on a computer, you know about drawing lines and the intended path for the ball. Use this same technique on the golf course.

- **Radar screen:** a golfer who worked for air traffic control told me that he stared at the blips on the radar screen all day long and when he did his visualization exercise on the putting green, he could see the blips of the radar creating a path all the way to the hole.

- **Stop-action photography:** a professional photographer who specialized in sports and action shots, saw the strobe effect of the ball traveling along its path into the hole. In other words, he visualized a line of golf balls leading into the cup.

- HOW TO READ GREENS -

14

How to Visualize What You Can't See: Draw the Line

For those students who tell me that no matter how hard they try, they just can't seem to *see* a line, I usually ask them the following question. "If you were to guess how the ball might get into the hole, what might that look like? If the putting green was a chalk (or white) board and I gave you a piece of chalk (or dry erase marker) to draw a path, what might you draw?" Every person has come up with some sort of path.

To train yourself and enhance your visualization skills, take your putter and hover it along the path your ball might follow into the hole. Another way is to use your finger and trace the path of the ball in the air from start to finish. When you use any of these techniques, you're visualizing a line. Visualization need not be complicated.

Now if you still have no clue and still don't *see* a line, make it up. Fake it. Imagine someone is willing to pay you $1,000 to just make up a line, any line. You'd do it right away. Whatever you come up with is a path and more often than not, a pretty good visualization. Then go for that line with 100% trust and commitment. You will make a more confident putt and give yourself the highest probability of getting it in the hole.

Some people are not visual. In other words, they use their other senses to determine the line or path of the ball. Some people have the ability to determine the path spatially. You often see people walking about the hole and their ball. By doing so, they can sense the differences in elevation and slope which helps them determine the ultimate path of the ball. Some have tactile acuity and can touch the green with their hand and get a sense for the contours of the green and how the ball might travel on it.

Choose any method that works for you. The key is that you use your chosen method consistently before every single putt.

- HOW TO READ GREENS -

15

How to See the Big Picture: Big Picture, Little Picture

When people are visualizing a putt or a shot on the fairway, they often get tunnel vision. Most would say that it's a good thing to block out everything and focus specifically on your target. I would agree, however, only after seeing and observing the big picture first.

For example, if you hold this book too close to your eyes, the words become blurry. You need to move it away to a certain distance so that your eyes can focus on each word.

Many times I see a student hit a putt that they think will be straight, but it ends up breaking one way or the other. At that exact moment, they seem perplexed.

I ask him or her, "Show me the line that you visualized."

The usual answer I receive back is, "I saw a straight line."

However, when we explore the decision-making process, it reveals a shortfall. It turns out that the visualization was limited to a very narrow space surrounding the hole. In other words, they were focused on too small of an area and lost sight of the big picture.

If you look too closely at the area surrounding the hole, it may look flat. However, when you look at a broader area around the hole such as the entire green and the hills and mounds around the green, you may notice something different. By looking at the big picture, you will have a better idea of the overall slope and contour of the green.

You may notice that the green slopes gently from left to right. You miss this important information when you focus too closely around the hole. Once you see the big picture, bring your focus to the immediate area about the ball and hole and determine your path.

The big picture, little picture approach will allow you to make a better decision. It's analogous to paintings. When you look closely at a small part of a painting, you see brush strokes, blurry lines and dots. However, when you step back and take a broader view, you observe the entire picture that was intended. Remember this when visualizing on the golf course.

16

How to Turn It On and Off: Flip on the Light Switch

When you watch one of the world's top golfers preparing to hit a shot, he or she goes through the same motions and actions leading up to the swing. Each individual has his or her own individual pre-shot routine or ritual. By doing the same thing before every shot, it helps accomplish several things: 1) it helps a golfer focus on the shot, 2) it gets the golfer into his or her own personal rhythm and 3) it eliminates extraneous thoughts and distractions. If you're not using a pre-shot ritual currently, it's time to start. If you are using one, it's time to perfect it.

The key to the whole ritual is the *beginning*. You need to separate and isolate each and every shot on the golf course. In a typical four-hour round of golf, how much time do you think you actually *play* golf? That is, swinging the club and hitting the ball.

The average golf swing takes about two seconds. If you multiply that by an average score of 90, that makes 180 seconds, which equates to three minutes. In other words, while you are out on the golf course for four hours, you are only playing golf for three minutes.

What do you suppose you are doing for the three hours and fifty-seven minutes of down time? Perhaps you are looking for your ball or your playing partner's ball. Some golfers spend every spare moment analyzing and criticizing their swing. Others are checking email on their smartphones or thinking about something off the course, such as work or family obligations.

The start of your pre-shot ritual is the key to separating being on the golf course from actually playing golf. When it's your turn to hit your shot, use a physical cue or trigger at the beginning of your pre-shot ritual. For a shot on the tee or fairway, I take my club and point it towards the sky on the trajectory and direction of my desired shot. When I do this, I am saying to myself, "Now I am playing golf."

It's as if I flip on a light switch. Once I do that, the light is on and it's time to focus. Determine some sort of personal trigger that you can use. By doing so, you will instantaneously elevate your body and mind to a higher state of focus and concentration. It's as if you're snapping your fingers and triggering yourself to attention.

Think of live television. When the red light on top of the camera turns on, you're on the air. It's show time. Think about the golf shot from that perspective. When it's your shot, it's your time. Create a trigger and use it to achieve a whole new level of focus.

17

How to Eliminate Distractions: STOP

How difficult can golf be? It's not as if there's an opponent out there trying to distract you or block your shot, right?

Even though direct opponents and noisy crowds do not necessarily exist in golf, there are still many distractions. Two types of distractions exist: 1) external and 2) internal. External distractions can be any type of movement or sound that may distract a golfer, such as a leaf blowing in the wind, someone yelling "Fore!" or a bee landing on your ball when you're about to swing. Internal distractions are thoughts that may distract a golfer, such as self-criticism, self-doubt, swing thoughts or off-the-golf course concerns such as work. Both types of distractions have the potential to negatively influence your overall performance.

I advise golfers to eliminate ALL distractions to play their best golf. At times this can be challenging. Some playing partners are constantly moving and talking. Wind and other types of natural elements can throw off your concentration. Stress and life's normal everyday commitments are constants.

It can be difficult to block out all distractions for a four-hour round. However, the only time I recommend golfers attempt to focus and concentrate and eliminate all distractions is when it counts—when it is time to hit a shot.

Concentrate for seconds, rather than hours. As mentioned in Mental Golf Trick #16, it takes only two seconds to swing and a few seconds to prepare for the swing. The key is to focus intensely only during the time just prior to and through impact with the ball.

When it is time for your shot, eliminate all extraneous thoughts and to the best of your ability ignore any external distractions. If at any point during your pre-shot ritual and swing, you become distracted, STOP. Then return to the beginning of your ritual and start again.

One of the tests I use in my golf academy is to walk about a student while he or she is in the middle of a pre-shot ritual and/or shot. If the student noticed me moving about, then they failed the test.

At first most say, "I noticed you a little, but it didn't bother me."

If a golfer notices even the most minor distraction for but a fraction of a second, it is more than enough to throw off his or her rhythm, timing and ensuing shot. Any distraction, however small and seemingly insignificant, is a major distraction. When you get distracted, stop and start over again. You will give yourself a higher probability of hitting your best shot.

18

How to Eliminate Swing Thoughts: Think Smooth

I enjoy observing golfers when they are about to hit a shot. For some, I can read them like an open book. As they stand over the ball preparing to hit a shot, I can almost hear them talking to themselves:

- "Bend the knees. Head down. Elbow in. Straighten the arms. Stick my butt out. Keep my eye on the ball. Don't look up."
- "Keep the club on plane. Turn my hips. Release my arms."
- "Oh no, the course marshal is watching. Don't screw up. Am I playing slow? The group behind is waiting. I better hurry up."
- "Watch out for the lake."
- "OB, don't go left."
- "Two down with two to go. I'm blowing this. I need to make this putt to stay in the match. I can't believe I'm losing."
- "This is embarrassing. I'm playing so lousy. I'm better than this. Not my day. I can't get it going. I should've stayed home."

At some point, I think all of us have said a few of these things to ourselves while standing over the ball. Rarely, if ever, have these swing thoughts helped us play better.

I often get asked the question, "What should I be thinking when I'm hitting a shot."

My answer? Nothing.

Many of my students tell me that it is difficult for them to think of absolutely nothing. If you are unable to keep your mind totally quiet, keep your swing thoughts to a minimum. In fact, keep it to one simple *qualitative* thought. Qualitative thoughts are descriptive rather than instructional or mechanical. I like swing thoughts like *let it go, swing free, easy does it* or *go for it!* By using these and other swing thoughts such as *smooth, easy,* or *relaxed,* you are subconsciously communicating those thoughts to your body.

If you have mechanical swing thoughts such as *straight arm, elbow in,* or *swing inside out,* you actually confuse your body. More than likely, your body will attempt to incorporate physical movements that cause your muscles to tighten up, often leading to a spasmodic, rigid and unnatural swing.

The body doesn't have enough time to respond to your physical directives and commands during the two seconds it takes to swing a golf club. Allow your body do the work without interference. Save the mechanics and tinkering for the driving range and practice green. If you must have a swing thought when you play golf, use a qualitative one to free up your swing and your game.

19

How to Stop the Bleeding: Hit Your Go-to Club

In my golf clinics, I stress the importance of practicing the way you want to play (see Mental Golf Trick #48). Many people go to the driving range and beat ball after ball until they're exhausted. I believe there are times to practice shots over and over again until you hit it perfectly. However, you never get the opportunity to do that on the golf course. One shot—that's it. You don't get a second chance.

So, if you're in a funk on the driving range, learn how to work through it. For example, if you start to slice or hook or top your driver while you are practicing, try to work through it. See if you can shift your performance. Take a water break, clean your club and then go through your pre-shot ritual as if you are on the golf course and see if you can change gears. If you can do it on the driving range, then you'll be able to do it on the golf course.

I've seen some pretty good golfers lose their swing quite abruptly. Perhaps they start a clinic by hitting some nice shots, then all of sudden they begin to shank it. It's as if they were jolted by an electric fence. It can then get worse as the internal analysis begins. Grips get tighter, the swing becomes rigid and the bottom falls out.

At this stage, a golfer can become so frustrated that he or she is ready to throw the club (which, at some times, might actually go farther than some of the shots). View this as an opportunity. Work through these hard times. If you can do learn how to do it on the driving range, then you'll be better equipped to do it on the golf course when it counts.

One mental golf trick I like to use in these situations is the *go-to* shot. When all else fails, go with the most consistent shot you can hit. For me, it's a little knockdown punch with my pitching wedge. If I had to, I could play the whole round with this one shot.

Determine the shot that you *know* you can hit well. It could be any type of shot with any club. When you seem out of sync on the range, grab the go-to club and hit the go-to shot. After hitting a few of these shots, gradually return to hitting other clubs. This approach will ease you back into your swing and get you back on track.

When on the golf course, you can also apply this trick even if it's not the ideal club to hit. Once you make that solid contact, your body and mind will remember the feeling of a great shot. Sometimes that's all it takes to shift gears.

20

How to Find Your Swing Mid-Round: I've Got Rhythm, You've Got Rhythm

I worked with a client who had played college basketball and was a skilled tennis player. He also had a beautiful flowing golf swing that was in balance from start to finish. However, that was only during his practice swing. When I put a little white ball in front of him, he developed a hitch-and-jerk motion. It was like day and night.

There was a deep disconnect between his practice swing and his actual swing. The difference was his attachment to outcome during the actual swing. Instead of letting the swing unfold naturally and intuitively, he began to think about what he was doing mechanically and how that would affect the result.

At some time in the past, he must have hit a shot using the hitch-and-jerk swing that led to a positive result (i.e., nice ball flight, the ball ending up on the green). Thinking it might lead to more of the same results, he continued to repeat the swing. It became a habit. However, the number of good shots became few and far between as time went on.

I gave him a little trick to get rid of the hitch-and-jerk motion and return to his beautiful *practice* swing. I told him to envision a swing that was musical. In other words, imagine a swing that flowed effortlessly and easily to the rhythm or tempo of a song. I told him to hum a tune in his mind or count 1-2-3 as if he was doing a little dance.

By focusing on rhythm, tempo and flow, it took his analytical left-brain thinking out of play and allowed the creative movement of the right brain to take over. Don Ho used to hum "Tiny Bubbles" when he swung a club. Many top golfers use a similar trick to help them maintain fluidity in their swings. Pick a tune that mimics the swing rhythm you desire and use it when you need to find your swing on the golf course.

21

How to Shoot Par on the First Hole: Drive...the Car

Most people think a round of golf starts with the first tee shot. To me, it starts long before that. Many of the top players of all time would spend the previous evening planning out their strategy for the next day's round. You will rarely find a professional player stepping up to the first tee cold without warming up at the driving range, chipping area and putting green. In today's golfing world, many workout or exercise prior to playing in a competitive round, as it helps them loosen up their bodies and leads to a more relaxed mind.

The realities of life do not always allow the regular player to spend hours in preparation for a round of golf. However, preparation for a round can start before reaching the first tee. As I'm driving to the golf course, I begin to plan out the first hole. I imagine the shots I want to create. Then in my mind, I select the ideal club and see myself hitting the ball to ideal locations.

If it's a golf course that I haven't played before, I picture myself on my home course hitting different types of shots on command. For example, I imagine myself hitting nice, high controlled shots off the tee. I picture myself hitting a low-boring draw around a dogleg left. I visualize myself hitting crisp irons toward my target on the green. I see myself hitting high, soft shots out of greenside bunkers. I see smooth and accurate chip shots into the hole. I imagine every putt going into the cup.

To shoot par or better on the first hole and to set the tone for a great round, lay down the groundwork while you're driving to the course.

22

How to Play 18 Great Holes: Maintain Your Energy

Four hours. Or more. The typical length of time to play a round of golf. Add in another 30-60 minutes for driving to the golf course, warming up and waiting to tee off. By the time you reach the 18th tee, it could be five or more hours that you have gone without eating or drinking. If you didn't eat before heading to the golf course, this time could be even greater. It's no wonder why so many golfers run out of energy by the time they reach the 12th hole.

You must keep your energy going throughout the round. No doubt, golfers burn calories and get dehydrated before and during a round of golf. Always have a few energy bars, bananas or other nutritious foods in your golf bag. You can also buy food from the beverage cart (though it might not be around when you need it the most).

The mental golf trick that I use is to have a snack and drink every four holes. If I had a meal within one hour of my tee time, I'm good to go. If it's been longer than that, I start my round with half an energy bar. I then eat a snack and drink water (or a drink with electrolytes) on the 4th, 8th, 12th and 16th holes.

It doesn't have to be a huge meal, but just enough for you to maintain your energy throughout the round. Too many highs or lows in your body will affect the quality of your game. Determine your ideal amount of food and drink and then the ideal time interval in order to keep your energy at a steady, consistent level. Then stick to the plan.

23

How to Play Business Golf: Flip the Switch

This mental golf trick is useful whether you play business golf or not. It is designed to help you play great golf when golf is not the primary purpose of your outing.

For example, whenever you are playing business golf, there is a dual purpose. One is to relate to your client, customer or business associate. The other is to play golf. Many of my corporate clients explain how difficult it is to focus on satisfying and catering to their customers needs and still play decent golf.

The key is to switch back and forth between business and golf throughout the round. Separate the experience into two distinct events. Event #1 is golf. Event #2 is business (or the social interaction or any other purpose for being on the golf course other than golf). Switch back and forth. When it is your turn to hit a shot, think to yourself "Event #1: Golf." After you hit the shot, say to yourself "Event #2: Business."

With this trick you will be able to focus on the task on hand with total dedication. You'll not only conduct your business successfully, you'll play great golf, too.

24

How to Close Out the Round: Send in the Closer

Many golfers reach the 14th or 15th hole in a position to post a great score. They play solid golf throughout the round and keep a nice flow to their game. However, during the last stretch of holes, they tend to collapse. Perhaps fatigue or loss of concentration or a lack of energy (see Mental Golf Trick #22) are the cause. If this has happened to you, it is the time to call in the *closer*.

In baseball or softball, every team has a closer. He or she is the pitcher that comes in fresh at the end of the game for only a few outs to secure the victory. When you reach the last few holes, it's time to call in the closer. Don't allow distractions such as the thought of shooting your best score or hanging out at the 19th hole pull your attention away from the task at hand.

In your mind, the manager is calling you (the closer) and giving you the ball to finish the game. There's no time to warm-up or get acclimated. The time is now. Focus your mind, body and energy towards successfully closing out the round.

25

How to Play Like a Pro: Trust and Commit 100%

Many golfers judge the quality of their shots by where their ball ends up. For example, if the ball goes in the hole then they must have hit a good putt. If the ball ends up on the green, they must have hit a good shot. However, this is not always the case.

I suggest measuring the quality of your shot not by where the ball ends up, but rather by the level of trust and commitment to your shot. In other words, if you hit the shot the way you intended to hit it, even if it ends up out of bounds, then that was a good shot. This may be a difficult concept and philosophy to adopt. Let me explain further.

Let's say that you are 110 yards from the hole and in your mind, you visualize the entire path of the ball (going up into the air, landing at a specific spot on the green, bouncing twice and then rolling into the hole). You pick one of your favorite clubs and commit to the shot 100%. The ball follows the path you visualized and lands precisely at the spot you chose. However, you did not realize that the spot you visualized is actually a sprinkler head and your ball hits it and bounces high into the air, over the green and into a sand trap.

Would you consider that a good shot? I hope the answer is, "Yes!" To me, you not only hit a good shot, you hit a fantastic shot. Why? Because you had total trust and commitment and hit the ball exactly as you desired. If you swing without doubt or reservation, then in my opinion, you have achieved a great shot, no matter where the ball ends up.

The outcome of the shot (what happens after you strike the ball) is out of your control. Nobody knows what the ball will do once it's in the air or when it lands or rolls on the ground. We're not in a vacuum when we play golf. The air is inconsistent and the ground is uneven. None of these factors are controllable.

All we can ask of ourselves is to fully commit to the shot we want to create. With this philosophy, good shots usually follow. Even if the outcome is less than hoped for, commend yourself for committing to your plan and move on. Reinforce the positive things you accomplish, knowing that in the long run it will pay off. This is how you can begin playing like a pro.

PART II

ON THE DRIVING RANGE & PUTTING GREEN

26

How to Get More Distance: Batter Up

Golfers will always seek more power and distance in their game. To accomplish this, many think they need to swing harder. However, this does not necessarily translate into longer shots. Many often lose their balance when they swing too hard, which leads to inefficiencies and shorter distances.

Rather than swinging harder, try this simple mental golf trick that will help you hit the ball farther with the same or even less effort. Plant your back foot into the ground as if you are a baseball or softball player in the batter's box. If you've ever seen someone at bat, he or she digs the back foot (right foot for right-handed players or left foot for left-handed players) deep into the dirt. This helps create a strong, firm foundation. That back foot becomes a brace or pushing off point.

When you see the player swing the bat, the transfer of energy and power starts from the back foot. He or she never rolls that foot away from the pitcher. If the player did, he or she would lose all the power.

The same goes for a golfer. If your back foot rolls

away from your target, it will be virtually impossible to shift your weight back toward the ball. This causes a golfer to lose his or her center and as a result, creates a weak shot.

Plant your back foot into the ground and make sure it stays set through impact. For some, it helps to keep that foot firmly planted until the follow-through when weight shifts to the forward foot. If you feel your back foot beginning to roll sideways away from the ball, that's a sign to improve your footwork.

27

How to Hit the Sweet Spot: Point-to-Point Contact

There seems to be a lot of hype regarding club head speed. Golfers try all sorts of exercise clubs, training aids, and workout regimes to help increase their speed. However, if the club misses the ball, club head speed is not going to help achieve the shot you want. Speed is not the only thing that matters. Contact is of equal, if not greater, importance.

We have all heard about the sweet spot. It's the part of the clubface that is designed to produce the best shots. When you hit the sweet spot, you maximize the transfer of energy from the club to the ball. Any contact that is off center or away from the sweet spot distributes that energy in other directions, which often results in shots that are not ideal.

By hitting the ball with the sweet spot of the club, you give yourself the best opportunity to create the shot that you want. That being said, if you swing as hard as you can, but hit the toe of the club, more than likely you will not end up with your desired outcome. On the other hand, if you hit the sweet spot and swing in slow motion as if you are in time warp, you might not get what you want either.

It's a combination of the two (quality and quantity) that gives you what you desire most. Most golfers generate plenty of club head speed with their current swing. The part that they often lack is hitting the sweet spot. Take a look at each of your clubs and determine where the sweet spot is located. Shrink the sweet spot down to a single point.

The modern clubs being manufactured today are said to have larger sweet spots. Some even claim that the entire face of the club is a sweet spot. Perhaps the area that produces acceptable shots is larger, but there is truly only one point that is the sweet spot. Focus on that point.

Take a golf ball in your hand and literally hold it up to touch that single point on the club head. Notice how one small portion of the ball connects with one small portion of the club. When you hit golf balls, in your mind, focus on connecting that one small point of the ball with that one small point (sweet spot) on the club.

Start with putting. You may notice a difference when you hit the ball with the sweet spot of the putter. It will seem almost effortless and more than likely the ball will roll straighter and truer. Furthermore, it will sound crisp, *pure* as golfers often describe. Most importantly, you will feel the difference in your hands. Try this with chips, pitches, irons, woods and the driver. Not every shot will be perfect, but you will be able to tell the difference between hitting and missing the sweet spot.

The next time you attend a professional golf tournament, take a closer look at each player's golf clubs.

Many of the club heads have what appears to be a dot, about the size of a dime, in the middle of their irons. That's where they tend to hit the ball, right in the sweet spot. Be cognizant of the fact that the dot is the size of a dime and not a microscopic point. In other words, even the best players in the world don't hit the exact sweet spot or single point perfectly every time. However, they hit it more often than the average player.

Try this mental golf trick and begin to improve your contact and connection to the sweet spot. You may realize that swinging easy in combination with better contact yields the best results.

28

How to Keep Your Head Down: Use Your Ears

Every golfer enjoys watching the ball roll into the cup or take flight high into the air. However, this or the anticipation of seeing the ball roll or take flight can lead to what we all know affectionately as "lifting your head up." It's turning your head to see where the ball is going prior to actually hitting the ball. It is considered one of the biggest no-no's in golf and often results in a topped or thin shot. How often do you hear golfers telling their playing partners "Keep your head down"?

What ensues can be quite amusing. I've seen people tuck their chins to their chests as if they are trying to hold an orange under their necks. Some shrug their shoulders inwards as if they are trying squeeze into a small space. Others tighten up their neck muscles so much that their veins pop out.

When a golfer tries to keep his or her head down, he or she tends to tighten up the neck and shoulders and along with that, the entire upper body. The golfer may be able to keep his or her head down, but that doesn't necessarily allow for a better shot if the swing is restricted.

Instead of physically trying to keep your head down, try this mental golf trick which accomplishes the goal of stillness, while at the same time allows for a relaxed swing: *listen*.

Listen for the ball rattling into the cup.

Listen for sound of the club striking the ball.

After you hear the sound, then and only then, look all you want. If you focus on the sound, your head will naturally remain still and your body will be more relaxed, leading to a smoother swing.

29

How to Stop Slicing: Grip Tight, Grip Light

One of the questions that I get asked most often is, "How can I stop slicing?" This question is usually accompanied with visible frustration and a painful wince.

Most people tend to grip the club tighter than necessary especially when they want to kill the ball. They also do this when they feel nervous or pressured on the golf course. The fight-or-flight instinct kicks in and the hands tighten up unconsciously.

Tension in the hands trickles to all parts of the body—the forearms, shoulders, neck, back, and legs. It's a chain reaction. So, what may have started as a relaxed grip that leads to a tension-free swing can instantaneously become a rigid clench that leads to a stiff and jerky swipe, which often manufactures a slice.

Some golfers have a very difficult time relaxing their grip pressure, especially when they are in the heat of battle on the golf course. Some are just as tight on the driving range.

There are many technical and mechanical ways to fix a slice. However, some golfers have learned these methods and still slice. One of my favorite mental golf tricks for eliminating the slice is to squeeze the club as tight as possible, followed by relaxing the hands completely, followed by swinging the club.

It's amazing how people can maintain lightness in their hands throughout the swing using this trick. Try this out the next time you're on the range or more importantly when you're feeling a little pressure on the golf course (i.e., first tee jitters, water holes, competition). You might just eliminate that slice and even begin to draw the ball.

This technique can also be used to relax the entire body as well. When you are feeling stressed or anxious, you can tighten up a muscle for a few seconds and then release the tension. You can do this for all parts of your body, starting with your feet, calves, thighs working your way up to your neck and shoulders. This is a great technique to relax the entire body.

30

How to Sink Putts From Any Distance: Spiral Exercise

One of the best tricks to build confidence in yourself and your golf game is called the spiral exercise. On the putting green, start with a golf ball six inches from the cup. Set up to the ball, establish your balance, find your relaxed grip pressure and knock it in the hole. Then rotate the ball out to one foot and hit that in the hole. Continue to move the ball out six inches further for each successive putt spiraling around the hole.

If you miss a putt, repeat it again from the same spot until you make it and then move on. With this exercise you will gradually build confidence in your putting and end up sinking putts with ease from every distance and angle.

Many people feel anxious when they are a certain distance away from the cup, perhaps five feet or so. The spiral exercise will help you work your way up to that distance and then break through the five-foot barrier. With this exercise, you will most likely be more relaxed, comfortable and confident as you gradually progress from putt to putt. By the time you reach that five-footer, you might not even notice the distance and continue with the same confidence.

You can also apply this same trick to other parts of your game. For chipping, start close at around five feet and hit shots until you get one within one foot of the hole. Then rotate out to 10 feet and hit shots until you get a ball within two feet and so on. Determine your measure of success and shoot for that goal.

If you are having trouble between 40 and 80 yards, start with shots from 10 to 20 yards, then work your way up to 30, 40, 50, 60, and so on. This way you build up confidence in your shot making and move forward only after mastering a particular distance. This will help you hit solid shots more consistently and develop the confidence to do it on command.

31

How to Hit Solid Shots with Less Effort: Hit the Tee, Hit the Ball

The next time you're on the golf course, observe your fellow playing partners closely. Watch their practice swings. Then, watch their actual swings. Notice something different?

For many, the practice swing is beautiful. It's smooth, relaxed and balanced. If I were to film some of my students' practice swings and send the video to the Golf Channel, many could be used as a model or example of a perfect, prototypical swing.

However, when I place a little white ball in front of those very same students, many transform into their evil twin. Body language changes dramatically. Hands and forearms tighten up as does the rest of the body. What was an effortless, free-flowing swing becomes a jerky, disjointed and choppy motion.

I call this the *gap,* the difference between the practice swing and the actual swing. If golfers used their practice swing for actual shots on the golf course, they would most likely hit the ball better. Nothing changes physically between the practice swing and the actual swing. The only thing that changes is in one's mind.

To bridge the gap, use this mental golf trick. On the driving range, set up two golf tees about six inches apart. Place a ball on the second tee. Step up to the first tee and make a practice swing, hitting the golf tee as if it is a ball on the ground. Then, immediately set up to the second tee (the one with the ball) and make the same exact swing.

In other words, make a practice swing with the first tee and the same exact swing with the second tee (and ball). Replicate the same effort and feeling in your swing, rhythm and tempo. The only difference between the swings is that the second tee happens to have a little white ball on it. Use the same relaxed *practice* swing to achieve more consistency and to strike the ball more solidly.

32

How to Lower Your Handicap: Build an All-Around Game

Golfers tend to focus on the areas of the game that they like the most. Many step up to the driving range with a huge bucket of golf balls, tee up the first ball and without stretching or warming up pull out their drivers and begin whacking away. They hit an entire bucket with their drivers. These people love the long ball.

I agree that when you hit a perfect drive and watch it soar into the sky on a perfect trajectory, it is an awesome feeling. However, if you just practice hitting the driver or spend the majority of your time on it, you will limit your overall ability as a golfer.

If this is your favorite part of the game, I recommend working on it regularly, since the drive has been proven statistically to be a major determinant for success in golf. However, to take your game to the next level, develop an all-around game. Instead of hitting the driver or another favorite club at the driving range for the majority of your practice session, determine the areas of your game that require improvement and give those areas attention as well.

This begins with an evaluation. Determine which parts of your game demand improvement based on your last few rounds of golf. How was your chipping and putting? Perhaps your driver let you down. Maybe it was your mid-irons that were missing the greens. Once you realize what areas need improvement, concentrate on those shots during your practice sessions.

If you keep focusing and practicing only the shots and clubs that you like, they will continue to improve, however at the sacrifice of other areas of need. Use the two-thirds/one-third rule. Dedicate two-thirds of your practice sessions to need areas and one-third to areas of strength. If you hit 60 golf balls, 40 are for need areas and 20 are for areas of strength.

You can apply this rule to putting as well. If putts in the four to six foot range are most troublesome, spend two-thirds of your time practicing those and the other one-third on other distances. Balance out your practice sessions. This will lead to a higher level of play.

33

How to Perfect Your Putting Stroke: The Pendulum

Many golfers struggle with their putting stroke. They are constantly analyzing, criticizing and coaching themselves. Many try to keep the putter moving straight back and straight through. Others make up a personal formula that calculates the distance and translates that into a certain movement. A golfer might attempt to always move the putter three inches back and three inches forward for a three-foot putt. At times, this can become so confusing and restrictive that the golfer loses his or her touch, feel and intuition.

To remind yourself of how simple this game can be, hold your putter at the top of the grip between your thumb and forefinger. Then put it up against your chest. Use your other hand to lift the club to the side and let go. Notice how the club simply flows side to side like a pendulum. A perfect, unencumbered motion.

Putters are designed to make a perfect stroke. We, as golfers, get in the way. Keep the image of the pendulum in your mind as you putt. Let the club do the work and simply go along for the ride.

34

How to Chip Like a Pro: Get it in the Hole

There are many theories about and techniques for chipping around the greens. Rather than discussing mechanics in specific, I'd rather discuss your frame of mind or mental mindset when chipping.

Even the best players in the world miss greens. They are faced with situations that require an adept short game. The difference between top touring professionals and the average amateur is how they think about the chip shot.

Technique aside, top players attempt to hit the ball in the hole. Amateurs just try to hit the ball. Though they don't make every chip shot, the touring professional holds the mindset of trying to hit the ball into the hole and that leads to higher quality shots.

When approaching a chip shot, visualize the ball flying in the air for a short distance, landing at a specific spot, and then rolling into the hole. By adopting this mentality for chipping and all of parts of your short game, you'll see a dramatic improvement in performance.

35

How to Hit Longer Clubs:
Choke Down and Swing It Like an 8-Iron

Many golfers view the 7- or 8-iron as their favorite club in the bag. Why? The length of the club is not too long or short, the weight of the club is easily balanced in their hands and the loft of the club head frequently creates high trajectory shots. Overall, these clubs tend to lead to a higher level of success, at least in the mind of the golfer. Success begets confidence and confidence begets more success.

If you hand golfers a long iron or fairway wood, often their demeanor changes dramatically. They become more rigid and uncomfortable. It's as if they are no longer familiar with the game of golf and are ill at ease. When they swing, their grip pressure seems to double in tightness and the smooth, easy going swing transforms into a jerky cut or swipe.

To hit your longer clubs with the same smooth rhythm and tempo of your favorite 7- or 8-iron, try this mental golf trick: select the longer club that you want to hit. Hold that club alongside your 8-iron with the club heads lined up side-by-side. After gripping the 8-iron, move your hands directly across to the other club and secure your grip.

You will be choking down (holding the club lower than the conventional grip position) and possibly holding the shaft. If you are holding the shaft, move your hands up slightly to the bottom of the grip. You are now effectively holding a club in your hands that is more similar in length to your favorite 7- or 8-iron. Proceed with your normal approach to the ball, but imagine swinging your 8-iron.

Armed with the mindset of using an 8-iron, swing easy. As a result, you will tend to strike the ball much better and connect with the sweet spot more consistently. If you were to take the average of 10 shots using this method versus 10 shots holding the club at the end of the grip, you might discover that this simple mental golf trick provides a better result overall.

This is a great way to get more comfortable and confident with longer clubs. It is also useful when playing in difficult course conditions or inclement weather (see Mental Golf Trick #11). By choking down, you gain more control. It is also useful when you're not at your peak physically. This technique will allow you to relax your swing and helps you make better contact.

As you get more comfortable and confident using this trick with your longer clubs, you can successively move your hands up towards the end of the grip and continue swinging with ease as if you have an 8-iron in your hands. Before you know it, you'll be able to hit all of your longer clubs as well as your favorite 8-iron.

36

How to Relax the Hands: Connect with the Club

The majority of golfers grip the club without conscious thought. Sometimes this can be good and sometimes this can be bad. Become more aware of the bond between your hands and the club. Notice how you hold the club. Notice the contour and texture of the grip. Notice the weight of the club in your hands. Notice how your hands intertwine. Notice how your fingers wrap around the club to touch your palm or another finger. Notice if your fingers overlap, interlock or do something else.

On a scale from 1 to 10, with 1 being feather light and 10 being the white-knuckle death grip, assess your personal grip pressure. When I teach large groups, such as executive teams and at golf tournaments, the distribution of grip pressures runs the entire spectrum. Usually there's one person who admits, "If I'm relaxed I'm at 9½, but usually I'm at 10. I like to have total control over my swing." Then at the other end of the line is the most relaxed person in the group and she says, "I hold the club very lightly at a 1, maybe a 2. I'm more relaxed that way." Which is right? Both. As long as the chosen grip pressure works optimally for the individual.

While there are a few at the extreme ends of the spectrum, the majority of golfers have a grip pressure towards the middle of the scale. At times, people seem confused by this exercise. Some seem to be waiting for me or another coach to tell them *how* to hold the club and with what grip pressure. We never do. We want everyone to discover his or her own. I recommend trying every grip pressure from 1 to 10 and determine which feels the best. Everyone is unique and thus, everyone will have a slightly different grip pressure. Discover your own perfect grip pressure and then maintain it consistently throughout the swing to play your best golf.

37

How to Lighten Up:
Find the Perfect Grip

Many golfers have told me how they discovered their perfect grip pressure using one of our exercises. However, for some it takes a mental golf trick or two to truly see if they have achieved what they think they have achieved. Most people's perception of their grip pressure is lighter than it actually is in reality.

Hold your club with your perceived ideal grip pressure. Make a mental note of the pressure on a scale from 1 to 10, as described in Mental Golf Trick #36. Once you establish your grip, ask a friend to hold the club head and gently pull the club away from you. Have him or her continue to pull gently as you gradually lighten your grip until the club begins to slip out of your hands. Once that happens, make another mental note of that particular grip pressure.

Perhaps you started with a 5 grip, but ended up at a 2 after this trick. Take a few practice swings with your new 2 grip. You may find that your hands, arms and upper body are much more relaxed allowing for a free-flowing swing. If you find the new grip pressure is too light to maintain throughout the swing, then experiment with grip pressures between where you started and the new grip (i.e., between the 2 and 5). Find a grip pressure that you can maintain consistently throughout the entire swing.

Many PGA, LPGA and Champions Tour professionals share how they attempt to hold the club as lightly as possible without letting go. I describe the perfect grip pressure as being "light, but not too light." This mental golf trick will determine if you're holding on too tight and give you the impetus to lighten up.

- HOW TO PERFECT YOUR GRIP -

38

How to Eliminate the Death Grip: Hold the Club Backwards

If you're having difficulty keeping a consistent grip pressure throughout your swing, this trick will help. Instead of holding the club the usual way, turn the club upside-down and grip the shaft near the club head. Hold it as if you were gripping the club normally, and swing.

This will accomplish a couple things. Because the shaft has a smaller diameter than the grip, you won't be able to hold it tightly. In fact, it may feel as if the club is simply resting in your hands. When you take a few practice swings, you'll be forced to hold the club lightly.

When you do this, you'll hear the club make a *whoosh* sound. The sound is created by the speed of the club moving through the air on your swing path. The sound will get louder through the point of impact, where the ball would be if you were hitting an actual shot.

Once you take a few swings as described and get into a nice rhythm, switch the club back and grip it normally. Then hit your next shot. You may find that not only is your grip pressure lighter and more consistent, but your rhythm and timing have improved as well.

- HOW TO PERFECT YOUR GRIP -

39

How to Get More Speed: Dangling Ropes

Tension in the arms and hands leads to a rigid swing and reduces club head speed. This prevents golfers from hitting their best shots and playing to their potential.

One of the most important principles that I emphasize is developing a feel or connection with the golf club. As mentioned, the majority of golfers grip the club tighter than is necessary. In fact, out of the tens of thousands of golfers that I have coached over the years, I can recall only two people who were better off with a tighter grip rather than a lighter one.

Ideally, you want to maintain the same grip pressure consistently throughout the entire swing. This allows you to swing evenly and smoothly. Some people have found it very difficult to do this. Many golfers may be able to start light, but by the time they reach the top of the swing or the point of impact, they are close to the white-knuckle death grip.

One trick I like to use and practice frequently is called *dangling ropes*. I imagine my arms are ropes and swing them around my body. I try to release all the tension and just let them whip around my torso such that they slap against my body. I do this until I feel my arms and hands are totally free of tension and control. Once I feel this, I know I am ready to start hitting golf balls.

This allows me to experience the feeling of keeping my arms and hands loose, like dangling ropes, which generates a lot of speed. Keeping them light throughout the swing allows me to hit more solid shots.

- HOW TO PERFECT YOUR BALANCE -

40

How to Get Balanced: Two-Foot Jump Stop

Balance is critical in golf. This is perhaps the most overlooked part of the game. If you are off-balance ever so slightly during the swing, more than likely you will miss the sweet spot, which often results in errant shots.

Here's an easy mental golf trick I teach at my golf academy to help golfers find balance without thinking too much about it. It's called the two-foot jump-stop.

Take a few steps and hop onto both feet at the same time. When you do this, your knees will bend naturally, your bottom will drop lower and you will end up in perfect balance. This is the feeling you want to have when you're standing over the golf ball getting ready to hit a shot.

The two-foot jump stop is used in many sports, including basketball, baseball, volleyball, tennis, wrestling and skiing. It's a great way to find your center. Even if you've never done it before, give it a try. You will discover that your body has a natural instinct to find balance.

You may also realize that much of your body's

weight is concentrated on the ball of each foot after doing this exercise. This is ideal for most sports and especially golf. This is a position in which you are able to move efficiently in any direction—upwards, forward, backward, left or right. Imagine playing tennis, basketball or volleyball. Most of your body weight is on the ball of each foot when engaged in these activities.

What makes golf so challenging, as compared to other sports, is that you don't have the time or the opportunity to move your feet in an attempt to find your balance mid-swing. You must start in balance in order to have it throughout the swing. Keep this in mind as you set up for your golf shots.

- HOW TO PERFECT YOUR BALANCE -

41

How to Solidify Your Balance: Roots and Soft Cement

When you establish a strong foundation with your legs and feet, you give yourself a great chance to generate a solid golf swing. One of the best mental golf tricks to maintain a strong foundation is to imagine the spikes in your golf shoes growing into the ground like the roots of a tree. The roots not only go down, but they spread underground, helping you create a solid core or trunk. Take it one step further, by imagining the soles of your shoes sinking into the earth as if you are standing on soft cement.

As your feet and legs get rooted and cemented softly into the ground, your foundation solidifies and creates a strong base that generates great energy and power in the golf swing. This will help you maintain your balance and center throughout the swing resulting in more solid shots.

- HOW TO PERFECT YOUR BALANCE -

42

How to Keep Your Balance:
Use a Bungee Cord

Every person is unique. Athletic experience, balance and coordination differ for each individual. This is quite evident in the golf swing.

One client had trouble hitting consistent shots. Every now and then he'd connect and hit a great shot, but more often than not, he'd hit it thin or top the ball. He often lost his balance during the back swing.

Growing up, he played most sports and was quite athletic. He could make a full back swing and easily maintain his balance. As he entered his thirties and forties, he became less active. Because his body and flexibility had changed over the years, he needed to make an adjustment.

I told him to imagine a bungee cord connecting his belt buckle to the tee (or ground below the ball). With this mental imagery, he could still make his body turn and at the same time, stay connected. The bungee cord would stretch and lengthen and at the same time, it would stay connected to the ball.

As a result, he was better able to sustain his balance

throughout the backswing, turn, impact and follow-through. He also discovered that he didn't need as long a back swing as before to hit the ball well. As a result of staying centered and more balanced, his swing became more efficient. He leveraged his current level of flexibility to hit the ball better than ever.

- HOW TO PERFECT YOUR BALANCE -

43

How to Finish in Balance: Start with the End in Mind

To maintain your balance throughout the swing, you need to first know how it feels to be *in* balance. A simple mental golf trick is to "start with the end in mind."

On the driving range, instead of setting up to the ball as usual, set up as if you are at the *end* of your swing. In other words, get into the ideal finish position. When you are in this position, make sure you are in balance with the weight on the forward foot as if you had just completed a perfect swing. Imprint this ideal finish position into your mind and body.

From the finish position, begin your back swing and then complete the entire swing as usual. The goal is to end up in the same finish position that you started with, maintaining perfect balance throughout. This mental golf trick will smooth out your swing and teach you how to finish in balance.

44

How to Optimize Your Swing: Swing Under the Trees

Top golfers maintain their balance throughout the entire swing. Even those with long back swings that go past parallel are able to stay balanced through impact.

John Daly has been described as a golfer with a long backswing. However, he could always maintain his balance during the entire swing. Arnold Palmer was always described as a golfer with a go-for-it, attack-like swing that looked out of balance and yet, it worked for him because he kept his center through impact.

Many of my clients ask me, "How far should my backswing go?"

It's different for each individual depending on flexibility and coordination. If you are extremely flexible, then you can use a longer backswing. If you are not as flexible, then you might benefit from a shorter backswing. The key is to maintain your balance.

I worked with a gentleman who had several fused vertebrae, which limited his rotation and flexibility. He wondered how he could keep playing the game he loved so much. I told him to take the club back just to the point where he could still be in balance. By doing this, he realized that he could also eliminate tension and tightness in his body, which resulted in a higher swing speed and ultimately more distance. He said he had never hit the ball so solid.

Many golfers still find it difficult to shorten their swing to an ideal length. One mental golf trick is to imagine standing under a tree with low hanging branches. If you were to use your regular back swing, you would hit those branches on the backswing. Thus, shorten the swing a bit. Try this little trick, and you might find that your swing becomes more efficient and your ball striking improves dramatically.

45

How to Groove Your Swing: Close Your Eyes

One of the best tricks to help you develop a good feel for your swing or putting stroke is to practice with your eyes closed. Many of you may be thinking, "What can that do for me? I'm not going to play with my eyes closed so why should I practice it?"

I encourage all of my students to try this "eyes closed" mental golf trick. It helps you become more attuned to your swing. We have five senses; we see, taste, smell, feel and hear. When you shut down one sense, the others become more acute. In other words, if you close your eyes, your other senses become more sensitive in order to compensate.

One of the exercises I have my students practice is hitting putts successively from one foot, then two feet, then three, four and five feet. Then I have them shift to another side of the cup and repeat the exercise. On the fourth set of putts, I have them do the same exercise, but before hitting each of the five putts, I tell them to close their eyes.

Surprise and amazement usually follow:

- "I can't believe I just made a five footer with my eyes closed!"
- "I'm putting better with my eyes closed than with my eyes open!"
- "I'm going to start putting with my eyes closed all the time!"

Putting with your eyes closed teaches you to develop more trust and feel in your stroke. When your eyes are closed, you eliminate distractions. You also quiet the inner critic that observes and judges what you are doing. As a result, you simply trust and let go. It's a leap of faith at the moment of impact.

Another time to use this trick is when you're rushing to the golf course for a tee time. We have all experienced arriving at the golf course with barely enough time to slam the trunk of the car and run to the first tee. With busy lives, we don't always have time to hit a bucket of balls or spend time chipping and putting before a round.

At times like this, before you are about to tee off, take a few practice swings with your eyes closed. This will give you immediate feedback on your swing, in regards to your balance, feel, timing and rhythm. More importantly, by taking a few swings with your eyes closed your body will start to self-correct and adapt until you find your groove.

This is also a great trick to use on the golf course in between shots, especially when you feel as if you aren't hitting the ball well. It will allow you to smooth out your swing without making too many mechanical or technical changes.

46

How to Have Fun: Beginner's Mind

I really enjoy coaching juniors. They have what I call *unhindered abandon*. They focus on one thing—having fun. Having fun means HAVING FUN. Rarely do young people think about how to hold or swing the club or how they look when they do it. They just play.

This is a powerful lesson for the adult golfer. There are certain times for drills and exercises. However, spend some time during every practice session, and hopefully every round of golf, just playing.

Be a child. Adopt the beginner's mind. Imagine it's your first time playing golf, step up and do it any way you want. Ignore your inner voice that says "I've got to get my swing plane just right" or "I have to hit it with a steeper angle." Try anything that seems like it might be fun. Try rotating your club in your hands and hitting lefty instead of righty (or vice versa).

Rediscover how much fun golf can be and try to do this regularly.

47

How to Not Get Bored: Playing Golf on the Range

When you are at the driving range warming up for a round of golf, instead of just hitting pointless shot after shot, hit the shots you might encounter on the golf course. "Play" the first few holes or a selection of holes or even an entire round of golf as if you are actually on the golf course.

Imagine yourself on a particular hole and visualize the shot you want to create. Then select the appropriate club and hit it as if you're on the tee or fairway. Next, imagine yourself at a spot in the fairway where you would ideally play your next shot. Continue with the process.

If you hit a shot that doesn't do what you intended, imagine hitting your next shot from where the ball might have ended up, like behind a tree. Play the next shot according.

If there is a particular hole on the course that has given you trouble repeatedly, make sure you play that hole to perfection on the driving range. If there is a hole that you know you can score well on, play that hole to reinforce your confidence. If you are a slow starter, play the first three holes. If you fade at the end of a round, play the last three holes.

If you are unfamiliar with a golf course that you are about to play, refer to the scorecard or yardage guidebook for the design and length of each hole and play a few holes on the range based on that information. At the very least, play the par-3 holes by noting the length on the scorecard and hitting the club(s) that you might use on those holes.

48

How to Go From Range to Course: Practice the Way You Want to Play

Often, I see golfers on the driving range hitting a huge pile of golf balls like a machine gun, rarely pausing between swings. At times, they achieve great rhythm and begin to hit each ball solidly.

When they get into a flow, I walk up and say, "Wow, you're really striking the ball well."

"Yeah, it feels pretty good," he or she may respond.

Then I ask, "How often do you get to hit balls like that on the golf course?"

"Never."

There are certainly times to practice the same shot over and over. However, remember to always take a portion of your time at the driving range to practice the way you want to play on the golf course. In other words, hit range balls as if you are actually on the course as mentioned in Mental Golf Trick #47.

This is powerful. By practicing the way you want to play, you are setting yourself up for success on the golf course. Create scenarios in your mind that you might encounter during a round of golf to make the impact even more powerful. For example, imagine yourself needing a par on the challenging 18th hole to shoot your personal best score. Step back and visualize the design of the hole with trees, bunkers and contours. The more vivid your imagery, the more powerful the effect.

Then play the hole. Select the club you would use, tee up your ball, step back and do your entire pre-shot ritual as you would do it on the golf course. Remember to do exactly what you would do as if you were playing a real hole.

If you are distracted during the pre-shot ritual, perhaps by a conversation in the next stall, stop and start over again. If you were on the golf course and got distracted, you would want to begin again. Practice the way you want to play. It will then become second nature when you're on the golf course.

49

How to Shoot Your Best Score: Go to Sleep

In Mental Golf Trick #21, I discussed how to shoot a par (or better) on the first hole by visualizing yourself playing each shot perfectly. Extend that to an entire round of golf. The next time you go to sleep, *play* or visualize the entire round in your mind shot by shot. If you are playing your home course or one that you are familiar with, see yourself playing each hole.

Picture yourself on the first tee, choosing your club, picking your target, going through your pre-shot ritual, making a smooth swing, seeing the ball take flight, landing, bouncing and rolling to your target spot in the fairway. Repeat this for every shot as if you are playing the perfect round. Choose the clubs, see yourself making the perfect swing, imagine the ball following the exact desired path and watch it end up at your target.

Folklore has it how a prisoner of war kept his wits intact by imagining himself playing his home golf course over and over again. It helped him maintain his sanity and focus. After several years of imprisonment, he was finally freed. He went home, played his home golf course and shot even par for the round.

Studies show how the body's physical and emotional states (i.e., heart rate, brain activity, adrenaline level) respond exactly the same whether doing an actual activity physically or by simply imagining it. By playing a great round in your mind, you are actually training your body to do it in reality.

50

How to Find the Perfect Swing: You Already Have It

I have yet to meet two people who are exactly alike. Even identical twins each have their own unique personality and style. Given this fact, it's funny how many people expect everyone to have the same exact swing. I find that hard to impose, especially with the physical, athletic, emotional and philosophical differences of each individual. To expect everyone to have the same interests in life is unrealistic. To expect everyone to have the same golf swing is unrealistic as well.

Each person has a dominant personality profile when they play golf. In the *Seven Personalities of Golf,* I talk about seven key personalities: the Intimidator, the Swashbuckler, the Methodologist, the Gamesman, the Steady Eddie, the Laid Back and the Artist. No personality is better than any other. However, each personality has its own pros and cons that can either help or hinder one's performance during a round of golf.

The key is to maximize strengths and minimize weaknesses of a particular personality profile at given moments and situations on the golf course. It is of equal importance to borrow from other secondary or non-dominant personalities to balance out your game. The premise of this concept is that everyone has his or her own unique style and to leverage that uniqueness. This extends to the golf swing as well as one's philosophy and approach on the golf course.

To me, the perfect swing is the one that fits you best. Every individual already has a perfect swing within him- or herself. It just needs to be discovered. This mental golf trick will help you do just that. At the driving range, try different types of swings that I describe as: smooth, easy, relaxed, fun, flowing, assertive, laid-back, rhythmic, natural, etc. Make up your own. By exploring different types of swing styles, you'll begin to gravitate towards the perfect swing for you. Once you discover your swing, use it on the golf course and remember that it is yours alone and has always been a part of you.

Parting Shot

I love the game of golf. I have a feeling that you do as well. There is really nothing like the feeling of hitting a golf ball perfectly and watching it go exactly where you want it to go. It doesn't happen every time, but it does happen.

The Frustrated Golfer's Handbook was written to encourage golfers of all levels to *never give up*. I want you to always remember that you have the potential to play your best on any given shot in any given situation. All it takes is a little trick here and there to coax you back into your own personal zone.

The great thing about golf is that every shot and every round is always a new experience. My wife often asks if I ever get bored playing the same course over and over again. I don't. Why? Because things are always changing—the course conditions, the weather, where the pins are placed. More importantly, I am always changing—physically, emotionally and mentally.

This is what makes golf a true challenge. We change not only day-to-day, but moment-to-moment. To be consistent in a sport like golf is very challenging, given the fact that we are changing constantly as individuals. These mental golf tricks are designed to help golfers retain, or regain, consistency using simple mental game techniques.

They work shot-by-shot. With these tools in the bag, any golfer can learn to hit desirable shots under any given situation. I hope they work for you and I hope they help you enjoy this game more than ever.

What's Your Best Mental Golf Trick?

If any of these tricks worked for you, or if you have a mental golf trick of your own, I'd love to hear from you. You can reach me at darrin@spiritofgolfacademy.com.

Turn the page for an excerpt from

The Seven Principles of Golf:
Mastering the Mental Game Off and Off the Golf Course

by Darrin Gee

Available now

Mastering the game of golf requires just as much mental preparation as it does physical practice. Yet few golfers devote adequate time or attention to perfecting what top mental golf instructor Darrin Gee calls the inner game— the game the golfer plays with the mind and the spirit. In *The Seven Principles of Golf*, Gee focuses on this absolutely central, if too often neglected, dimension of golf, sharing the essential principles he has derived from helping thousands of golfers—both amateurs and professionals— improve their game.

The Seven Principles of Golf are:

The First Principle: Get Grounded
The Second Principle: Develop Feel
The Third Principle: Visualize the Shot
The Fourth Principle: Create Your Own Pre-shot Ritual
The Fifth Principle: Find Your Natural Swing
The Sixth Principle: Play One Shot at a Time
The Seventh Principle: Transform Your Golf Game,
Transform Your Life

The First Principle of Golf: Get Grounded

"You can will something to happen, with your body, with your mind. The mind is that strong. You can say, `I want to get this close to the hole.' That's where the mind comes in. The mind has to produce positive thinking. All the great players do that."
Byron Nelson

Golfers take balance for granted. When my students set up for a golf shot, I frequently ask them if they feel balanced. After assuring me that they are as balanced as they possibly can be, I give them a gentle, two-finger nudge and watch them topple over.

Most people think that if they are standing still, they are balanced. However, this theory quickly falls apart during the golf swing. If a golfer has not established a strong, well-balanced stance prior to swinging the golf club, he or she will have a difficult time striking the ball crisply in the sweet spot.

In most other sports, a balanced athletic stance is also required. Whether it be volleyball, tennis, basketball, football, or martial arts, you must be prepared to move in any and all directions, almost reflexively. Not knowing where your opponent or the ball will be going, you must have perfect balance at all times to respond accordingly. We can use that same thinking when playing golf.

I had one student who was an accomplished athlete in many sports, including basketball, football, and baseball. He was strong, quick, and had outstanding hand-eye coordination. He demonstrated outstanding balance in every sport he participated in, *except golf.* When he addressed the ball, he was off-center, often leaning back on his heels. When he swung the club, he often finished out of balance, wobbling around while trying to remain standing.

Golf is a "still" sport. You are primarily stationary, which means that balance in golf is even more important than in other sports. In most other sports, if you lose your balance, you can move your feet to regain it and resume play. In the game of golf, the swing takes less than two seconds. In such a short period of time, you don't have time to move your feet and adjust. Shifting your entire weight from one side of your body to the other, without moving your feet, while swinging a golf club and trying to hit a tiny ball, is probably one of the most difficult motions in sports to master.

I believe that balance, or getting grounded, is the core and foundation of the golf swing. A golfer may have a beautiful, fluid swing, but if it's coupled with poor balance, the result is often an off-center shot. You must first establish a grounded, balanced stance as the basis for a solid golf swing.

•••

You often see professional golfers shuffling their feet around, rocking back and forth, and adjusting their stance in preparation for a shot. This is often misunderstood as a nervous habit, but more often than not they are just trying to find their balance and establish solid grounding before making their swing.

A student of mine named Don visited me at our golf academy, desperately wanting help with his golf game. He and his buddies had all started playing golf at about the same time. His friends seemed to improve, while he did not. He often felt embarrassed by his poor play and worried what others thought about him and his game. Compounding the situation, he doubted his golf swing and often found himself having a million different swing thoughts before, during, and after a shot. As a result, he often tightened up during his swing, hitting more dirt than ball.

Don had taken lessons, read golf instruction books and magazines, and tried several swing aids and gimmicks. He improved a little each time, but always regressed back to his original ability, sometimes even getting worse. Because of his struggles with the game, he nearly quit, until I shared with him a few things about quieting the mind, finding his balance, and trusting his body.

Don had a lot on his mind, both golf- and non-golf-related thoughts. He often rushed his shot in an attempt to "get it over with." He rarely took the time to establish a sound foundation. As a result, he often lost his balance during his swing and rarely made solid contact with the ball.

I asked him to get as balanced as possible as he set up to the golf ball. Once he said he felt balanced, I gave him a soft push on his shoulder. He nearly fell over. Don needed to improve his balance and learn how to ground his body.

First, I had him stand on his toes and lean forward, while maintaining his balance throughout his body. Then I had him lift up his toes and stand on his heels. This proved to be very challenging to him. I then asked him to rock back and forth, heel to toe, toe to heel, imagining that he was a rocking chair. This exercise helped him gain a better sense of balance and rhythm. I told him to slow down and shorten the rocking motion until he reached an equilibrium point between his toes and heels.

He then repeated the same exercise laterally, or sideways. Finally, I had him make small circles with his hips. As he was doing this, I told him to imagine circling around the center of his body. I told him to make smaller and smaller circles, spiraling until he reached the center point.

At this point, he had essentially found his center. However, this was not enough. In order to lock in this feeling of total balance, I told Don to imagine the spikes in his golf shoes growing into the ground like the roots of a tree. Using the imagery of roots growing down and spreading in all directions helped him establish a solid foundation. I had him put particular emphasis on the balls of his feet, which gave him a solid, grounded feeling.

I asked him to swing his arms back and forth around his body, while keeping his feet firmly planted. He built a strong foundation, and yet he was completely loose and flexible on top. Using the imagery of a palm tree or willow tree, Don was able to achieve a balance of strength and flexibility, exactly what is needed for the golf swing.

With his eyes closed, Don learned to maintain his balance and notice the difference between "thinking" he was balanced and actually "being" balanced. By focusing on his feet and legs being firmly rooted into the ground, he improved his swing dramatically. And yet his swing was essentially the same: what changed was his balance. What was once a swaying, imbalanced, and off-centered swing became a solid, flowing, and effortless motion.

I told him to close his eyes and practice his swing. He could immediately discern the difference between good and poor balance. When he concentrated on his feet and legs being rooted into the ground, he had better balance. If he thought of anything else, he lost his balance.

When Don started hitting golf balls after this exercise, he hit them with both precision and accuracy. His shots lofted in the air like he had never seen before. He was amazed. The First Principle of Golf, Get Grounded, helped Don focus on establishing a strong connection between his body and the ground, which led to solid swings.

•••

How is *your* balance? There are a few simple ways to test its quality. Standing on one foot with your eyes closed is an exercise that will give you feedback on your balance. Notice how you must adjust to find the perfect balancing point. You may wobble a bit, but this exercise will help you establish better balance for future golf swings. Remember to do this with each foot, as we often favor our stronger leg first. You want to feel so grounded that you would be able to maintain your balance on uneven lies and in gusty and windy conditions.

Making practice swings with your eyes closed will also help you find your balance. Notice how your feet and legs must work diligently to maintain your balance throughout the swing. This is no different when your eyes are open. Keep swinging with your eyes closed, until it feels smooth, rhythmic, and flowing. Then take a few swings with your eyes open and notice how your balance has improved.

Another way to achieve better balance is through an exercise called the two-foot jump stop. Used in almost all sports, including basketball, baseball, tennis, and volleyball, this exercise teaches you how to achieve a solid, balanced stance without trying or thinking. Take a few steps in succession followed by a short hop, landing with both feet on the ground simultaneously. Allow your knees to bend and flex naturally. You may find that when you land, you have the majority of your weight on the balls of your feet or slightly forward. Let your arms dangle. This is a very natural stance and perfect for the golf swing.

If you lean too far forward during this exercise, you'll fall over; if you lean too far backward, you'll get jolted back. With a few repetitions, this exercise will help you find perfect balance.

Turn the page for an excerpt from

The Seven Personalities of Golf:
Discover Your Inner Golfer to Play Your Best Game

by Darrin Gee

Available now

Featured in the July 2009 issue
of GOLF Magazine,
"The New Way to Manage Your Game"

Every golfer, amateur or pro, has a dominant personality: a set of traits that sometimes helps you win—but sometimes lands you in the rough. In this exciting new book, leading mental golf instructor Darrin Gee helps you identify which is your dominant personality and tells you how to use that information to play your best game yet.

The Seven Personalities of Golf are:

The Intimidator (Tiger Woods)
The Swashbuckler (Arnold Palmer)
The Methodologist (Nick Faldo)
The Gamesman (Lee Trevino)
The Steady Eddie (Tom Watson)
The Laid-back (Fred Couples)
The Artist (Seve Ballesteros)

THE SWASHBUCKLER

"The most rewarding things you do in life are often the
ones that look like they cannot be done."
Arnold Palmer

With the title of Swashbuckler, think of a pirate or
cowboy, who swoops in, with grace, style, and an aura of
confidence and charisma, to save the day. He or she does
this in such a charming way that all those who observe it
immediately fall for this person. The public feels this
golfer's emotions and experiences, his or her highs and
lows. That is perhaps why there is such an affinity for
Swashbucklers. We feel they are one of us.

On the golf course, the Swashbuckler seems to thrive
on risk and taking chances, even when the probability of
success is low. If there is an opening, however small, the
Swashbuckler will go for it simply because it exists.
These golfers don't weigh the odds and take the option
with the lowest amount of risk. They just go for it,
sometimes to their own detriment.

When they take risks and succeed, the triumph is
shared by all. If they fail, the pain is equally felt, and
perhaps even more so. In some ways, observers live
vicariously through the Swashbuckler. Because the
Swashbucklers wear their hearts on their sleeves, they
are universally admired by and endeared to the public.
We tend to identify more closely with this type of golfer.

They often possess more natural talent and skill than
their peers, but that does not always equate with more
victories and successes. They are gamblers in a way.

They see the world in black and white. Victory or defeat. No in-between exists.

It is quite typical for a golfer with a Swashbuckler personality to finish first. It is equally possible for this person to finish last. They are not necessarily consistent top-ten finishers. More often than not, they are all or nothing. This quality and approach to golf, and perhaps life, is so appealing to the golf fan. The Swashbuckler demonstrates an unsurpassed love of the game and a flair for excitement, risk, and thrill.

At times, the Swashbuckler applies his or her strengths to create the most amazing shots seen in competition. The Swashbuckler's high-risk, high-reward play is lauded and encouraged by his or her fans. These golfers are often followed by armies or swarms of people. And the groups of followers are diverse—young and old, men and women, seasoned low handicappers as well as non-golfers. The Swashbuckler has universal appeal.

Arnold Palmer fits this description. His "go-for-broke" philosophy combined with his boyish charm, charisma, and cowboy swagger was, and still is, irresistible to fans. Even today, he is arguably the most popular figure in golf, even though he has retired from the professional arena.

Arnold would keep it simple. As his father taught him, he would hit the ball as hard as he could, and then he would hit the ball as hard as he could. This attitude led him to tournament victory after tournament victory. But what set him apart from all the rest was not how many tournaments he won, but rather *how* he won them.

Oftentimes, when he was seemingly all but out of the

tournament, he would come from behind with high-octane energy and force. Trailing by seven strokes heading into the final round of the 1960 U.S. Open at Cherry Hills Country Club in Colorado, he boldly grabbed his driver and went for the green on the par-4 313-yard first hole. To the thrill of the crowd, he drove his ball onto the green and set the tone to achieve the greatest final-day comeback in U.S. Open history.

If you ever saw Arnold play golf, you know he rarely held back. His go-for-it philosophy served him well overall. In fact, most golfers who have Swashbuckler personalities play their best when they take risky shots. The thrill and excitement of pulling off a difficult shot is what gets them going.

I believe some of these golfers use the same traits off the golf course. They love and enjoy not only golf, but life as well. Swashbucklers are equally daring, and successful, in their business affairs. They do not necessarily show off their skills or achievements. It is simply who they are. They put all of themselves into every shot and every experience.

However, there are times when this philosophy can be a detriment. This type of individual could benefit from knowing when to tone down the go-for-broke personality. As mentioned in the introduction, Phil Mickelson's experience in the 2006 U.S. Open is an example of the Swashbuckler personality gone awry. He could have benefitted from toning down his natural approach and style.

For 99 percent of the time, Phil needs to play his Swashbuckler personality to perform at his best. He said in an interview that he needs to play a high-risk/high-reward game in order to have fun and enjoy golf and ultimately play his best. However, even Phil realized that he had to tone down that approach at times in order to win major championships, which he has done so successfully. If he had applied that philosophy to the 2006 U.S. Open, he would have had one more.

One of my golf academy clients named John was an extremely gifted twenty-five-year-old golfer with a flair for excitement. He called every shot or, in other words, he told me exactly what type of shot he was going to hit before he hit it. "I'm going to hit a high draw, starting out toward that cloud, and then turning about twelve feet to the left," he'd say prior to executing the shot. "Next, I'm going to hit a low-boring four-iron that will stay under the wind and roll forever."

No doubt he had the skills and, more importantly, the confidence and attitude to create the shots he described. However, when I took him on the golf course for a playing lesson, his Swashbuckler personality let him down at times, especially when we reached the 6th hole, a 404-yard par-4 with a large lake to the right of the green. The hole had one lone tree about 130 yards short of the green, fronting the lake. From the tee, the tree appeared to be in the middle of the fairway.

I described the hole and various strategies for playing the hole. If the tee shot went too long and right of center, the tree would block the approach to the green. If the tee shot went left, it would need to carry over 275 yards to fly the sand traps. The safe, high-percentage landing area that would give an unobstructed approach to the green would require less than a driver for John. What did John do?

His Swashbuckler personality got hold of him. He took his driver and attempted to fly the traps on the left, which was a stretch for him. He hit the ball far, with enough distance to clear the traps, but because he felt he had to swing a little harder, his ball faded slightly to the right . . . directly behind the tree.

On the next shot, he was too close to the tree to go over it, and the tree trunk was blocking the line to the green if he attempted to go under. Going to the right would take him over the lake and he would have to hook it at least fifty yards. The safe route would be to punch the ball left into the fairway to set up a third shot from seventy-five yards—a perfect sand wedge for John. What did he do?

Among the tree branches, he saw an opening about the size of a steering wheel. He couldn't help himself and took out an 8-iron. Amazingly, the ball headed right for the opening, but one tiny branch knocked it off line to rattle in the tree and drop into the lake. John was furious. He felt robbed. Now he was looking at double bogey or worse.

He never viewed this as a low-percentage shot per se. It was just a shot, and a fun one at that. The thrill of potentially pulling off the shot got the best of him. This would have been a good time for John to soften his dominant Swashbuckler personality and adapt to the conditions and situation at hand. By applying a more objective perspective instead of going with his initial knee-jerk reaction, John would have been able to make a more thorough evaluation of the risk and reward in each option. More than likely, he would have realized that he could punch out to the fairway, leaving him an unobstructed approach to the green. With his outstanding shot-making skills, he would then have had a high-percentage attempt to get the ball close to the hole, setting up the opportunity to save par.

SEVEN PERSONALITIES OF GOLF PROFILER

Determine if THE SWASHBUCKLER personality is your dominant personality by completing the following survey:

5 = STRONGLY AGREE
4 = AGREE
3 = NEUTRAL
2 = DISAGREE
1 = STRONGLY DISAGREE

1. ____ I have a "go for it" attitude.
2. ____ I like taking risks on the golf course.
3. ____ I have a vivid imagination.
4. ____ I consider myself a go-getter on and off the golf course.
5. ____ I like to imagine different types of shots from the same lie.
6. ____ I enjoy the thrill of attempting and achieving a difficult shot.
7. ____ I like playing a golf course for the first time.

8. _____ I enjoy courses with many hazards and challenges.
9. _____ I enjoy golfing with others rather than by myself.
10. _____ I enjoy playing games on the golf course.

YOUR TOTAL SCORE *(add up all ten answers and circle the correct answer below)* _____

40-50 DOMINANT PERSONALITY
30-39 SECONDARY PERSONALITY
0-29 NON-PERSONALITY

About the Author

Darrin Gee is the founder of the Spirit of Golf Academy, one of the most successful and innovative golf programs in the country. He is an expert in the field of mental golf and is one of the top mental game coaches today. Darrin has been featured in *Golf Magazine, Golf Digest, The Golf Channel, Travel & Leisure Golf, LA Times, The Boston Globe, The Chicago Tribune,* and ESPN Radio.

He is the bestselling author of *The Frustrated Golfer's Handbook, The Seven Personalities of Golf* and *The Seven Principles of Golf* as well as the bestselling DVD series, *Mastering the Mental Game of Golf.* Darrin has also appeared in *1,001 Reasons to Love Golf, The Secret of Golf,* and *Fifty More Places to Play Golf Before You Die.* He holds a BA in Psychology from UCLA and received his MBA from Northwestern University. He lives in Hawaii with his family.

If you'd like to get in touch, feel free to send an email to Darrin at **darrin@spiritofgolfacademy.com**. Hopefully he'll be on the golf course when he receives your email.

Darrin Gee's Spirit of Golf Academy

Darrin Gee's Spirit of Golf Academy is a golf instruction program located on the Island of Hawaii. The academy works with players of all levels from PGA and LPGA Tour Professionals to first-time beginners at several courses throughout the island. Darrin and his coaches are available for group, corporate or incentive meetings.

Darrin Gee's Spirit of Golf Academy was named one of the top golf schools in America by *Golf Magazine* and endorsed by PGA Tour Professional and three-time Tour Winner Jerry Kelly, who said, "The Spirit of Golf is essential to the game of the seasoned professional as well as the beginning golfer."

To learn more or to schedule a golf session, visit www.spiritofgolfacademy.com or call (808) 887-6800.

Acknowledgments

My thanks to the thousands of golfers who have joined us at the Spirit of Golf Academy. Your genuine excitement and enthusiasm continues to motivate me to create new and innovative ways to enjoy the game.

Much gratitude and appreciation to all my Spirit of Golf Academy coaches, past and present. Special thanks to Dave Young, Dan Skellan, Matt Hughes and Emily Gail, who not only share a common passion for the game of golf, but also the desire to inspire others to discover the same.

Made in the USA
San Bernardino, CA
28 July 2015